Crafting Strategy

Planning how you will

prevail over competitors

and obstacles

by Bob Frost, Ph. D.

Published by
Measurement International
P. O. Box 7848
Dallas, Texas 75209-0848

ISBN 0-9702471-0-9

Printed in the United States by:
Morris Publishing
3212 East Highway 30
Kearney, NE 68847
1-800-650-7888

Contents

Preface

This brief book outlines the evolving field of strategy for busy managers and executives. We take a comprehensive approach, yet simplify the field wherever we can and focus on the practical work to be done.

Crafting Strategy grew out of our work in measuring and improving organizational performance, where we saw the need for better materials to support strategy at the enterprise level and, even more, at the SBU and product levels. The resulting book is designed to address:

- **The essential concepts,**
- **The most useful tools**, and
- **The process** of crafting strategy.

In *Crafting Strategy* you have a primer to help prepare for productive work on strategy. We greatly respect the differences among businesses, so you will not find any one-size-fits-all approaches, nor any attempts to completely integrate all the different ideas about strategy. As you select the views and tools here that best apply to your situation, you will be taking the first step toward orchestrating a custom strategy process. From there, the details of how you craft your strategy, like the strategy itself, must be carefully tailored for your organization and circumstances.

– Bob Frost

Part 1

Introduction

- Strategy in Business
- The Work of Strategy

Strategy in Business

"Business more than any other occupation is a continual dealing with the future." —Henry R. Luce

Strategy is popular again. Perhaps too much so. People today commonly glorify the most ordinary activities as "part of our strategy" and describe even mundane decisions as "strategic." What is strategy and what is not?

Satisfying answers are elusive. As I write this, eleven well-known management books are stacked on the desk before me. Each takes a quite different slant on strategy, resulting in an overall picture that is sometimes more confusing than illuminating. Fortunately, the best works on strategy also have many points of agreement.

As one point of agreement, all insist that strategy differs from long range planning and that this distinction is too commonly lost. They note how successful enterprises can become too inclined to "stay the course"—allowing too much of their strategic planning to be replaced by forecasting and budgeting exercises based on extrapolated trend lines. To the degree an organization allows trend lines to short circuit penetrating analyses of markets, crucial trends, and competing in the future, it sets a perilous and vulnerable course.

Further Agreement. Most practitioners agree that *strategy is your plan for managing capabilities, resources, markets,* *competitors and obstacles in order to achieve your goals.* Thus, strategy is about five things:

1) Setting direction,

2) Long term success,

3) Competition,

4) Distinctive capabilities, and

5) Sustainable advantages.

At bottom, strategy is about achieving your ambitions and prevailing over competitors and obstacles. More specifically, it is about your plan for *how* you will prevail over competitors and obstacles.

The Practice of Strategy. Modern strategic planning came into business in the 1950's and grew rapidly through the 60's and 70's. Its focus on risk, industry growth, and market share complemented the "portfolio" thinking that developed as large conglomerates emerged. Then, in the 1980's, large U. S. corporations and their strategic business units (SBU's) faced a crisis. Suddenly, many seemed less agile and less competitive than those outside the U. S. They were accused of being overstaffed with middle managers, out of touch with customers, suffering from analysis paralysis and operating on a philosophy of

"Ready . . . aim . . . aim . . . aim" in a world where "Ready . . . fire . . . aim" seemed to be what worked. As many struggled to lose weight and gain agility, they put traditional approaches to strategic planning on the back burner. Way back.

Though traditional planning exercises were officially out of favor, these difficult times had important consequences for strategic thought at business unit levels. They brought a sense of urgency, a need for "street smarts," and significant executive involvement to strategy efforts that had too-often been staff exercises. Many were forced to seriously ask such questions as "What's really the core of this enterprise?" "What does the customer value?" and "How can we do more with less?"

> "Catching up is necessary, but it's not going to turn an also-ran into a leader."
> —G. Hamel & C. K. Prahalad

Great strides were made in focusing work efforts, managing work processes, eliminating non-valued activities, and facing up to the competitive environment that now characterizes business. Though we asked a lot of the right questions during this period and made great progress, in the end it became clear that the operational improvements we achieved, while essential to survival, weren't really sources of sustainable competitive advantage. Everyone else was achieving the same things.

8.

Where are we today?

1) Virtually all enterprises recognize that applying a strategy to beat competitors and overcome obstacles really counts.

2) Virtually all enterprises realize they must focus on the needs and wants of their stakeholders— especially their customers and stockholders.

3) Many enterprises again have people in key positions dedicated to strategy work.

4) Most enterprises set aside a specific time to renew their understanding of the business, its competitive position, and its direction for the future.

5) Many agree on the content of a strategic plan. The best ones refine the mission and goals of the enterprise, assess its internal strengths and weaknesses, assess the opportunities and threats in the outside environment, set forth initiatives to achieve a more advantageous competitive position, and establish feedback mechanisms of milestones and metrics by which strategy implementation will be tracked and adjusted.

Before moving on, let's return to our initial observation about the wide range of writings that all claim to be addressing the same topic, strategy. One reason these writings are so diverse stems from the fact that they discuss strategy in four different contexts—each slicing at a different organizational level: competitive strategy, business strategy, corporate strategy, and national strategy. The net effect is like the old story about three blind persons who each describe an elephant by touching a different portion of the animal. It's all one topic, but the parts of it differ considerably.

Competitive Strategy (or market-level strategy, or customer-level strategy) emphasizes the basis on which products and services vie for customers—price, quality, support, image, etc. or some mix of these.

Business-Level Strategy emphasizes competition across markets, positioning vs. competitors, market segmentation, creating and/or entering new markets, etc. Here, strategy is about capturing markets, winning competitive battles, controlling the basis of competition, and gaining sustainable advantages.

Corporate Strategy commonly addresses portfolio management, asset allocations, capability and competency management, inventing the future, race to execute, shareholder return, etc.

Discussions of strategy at the *National Level* (Grayson and O'Dell, 1988; Kay, 1996; Porter, 1998) emphasize how the policy decisions and investments of a nation (in education systems or communication infrastructures, for example) bear on its future competitive position and prosperity compared with others.

It's pretty easy to see that all these perspectives on strategy are valid, but that they also lead to quite different ways of describing the same elephant. Realizing this can help as you try to absorb the strategy literature.

In this book, we'll be addressing strategy primarily at the first two levels: customer-level competitive strategy and business-level strategy for an SBU or product group. A few corporate-level concepts are also included that bear on SBU issues; you will find no coverage of strategy at the national policy level.

The Work of Strategy

"The most common source of mistakes in management decisions is the emphasis on finding the right answer rather than the right question."   –Peter Drucker

Much of your success in crafting a strategy will result from asking and answering difficult questions about your business. Before that, it will require searching out the right questions to address. As we noted earlier, these questions focus on *setting direction, long term success, competition, distinctive capabilities,* and *sustainable advantages.* Let's catalog some of them:

Questions about direction:
- Are we in the right business for today?
- Are we in the right business for the future?
- Are we responding properly to emerging trends?
- What more should we be doing about emerging issues?

Questions about long term success:
- Do we have a vision of the future appropriate for an organization like ours?
- What is the long term condition of our franchise with customers?
- Are our distinctive capabilities right for the future?
- Given our present capabilities, what portion of future opportunities can we expect to capture?
- On what basis do we prefer to compete in the future?
- What are our long term prospects for creating value?

Questions about competition:
- Is our basis of competition right for us? What might improve our basis of competition?
- Do we compete against the right competitors?
- How can we combine new competitive advantages or protections with those we already have?
- Must we improve operational effectiveness to protect ourselves from those who are more efficient?
- Can we be price squeezed by suppliers or customers? How might we protect ourselves?
- Why are we better than others in creating value?
- How might our competitive position become more unique?

Questions about distinctive capabilities:
- What are our distinctive capabilities?
- Do our distinctive capabilities match our markets?
- What other markets are good matches for our distinctive capabilities?
- What is the longevity and future value of our intellectual property?
- What is unique about our people and their talents?
- What is unique about our business processes and practices and how they contribute value?

Questions about sustainable advantages:
- How might our competitive advantages be made more sustainable?
- What new competitive advantages could we create or acquire that would be more sustainable?
- What could reduce or eliminate our competitive advantage? How might these events be prevented?
- How might we control the competitive game through industry standards and other points of leverage?

13.

This catalog of questions is a sampler, and by no means complete—many others will be suggested by the circumstances of your situation. As a group, however, they say a great deal about the work of strategy. Strategy is about finding the right answers to questions like these. From here on, we will overview the concepts, tools, and processes by which you can, with diligent effort, find the right answers for your enterprise.

Part 2

_____

A Strategy Checkup

A Strategy Checkup

Are your current efforts in strategy producing the right results? Are they holding their own as part of your management process? Are they worth the time and effort you're investing? Let's look into what they're supposed to do and compare to what they're actually doing for you.

On the items that follow, rate the effectiveness of your strategy efforts according to this scale:

1 = No value on this goal
2 = Some help on this goal
3 = Quite helpful on this goal
4 = Extremely valuable on this goal

STRATEGY CHECKUP

_____ 1) Our strategy efforts result in a *clear picture* of our organization in the future.

_____ 2) Our strategy works as a coordinating, *unifying force* for us.

_____ 3) Our strategy process is *seen as relevant and valuable* by top executives and line managers.

_____ 4) All employees *know our basis of competition*, how we intend to get and keep customers.

_____ 5) Our strategic plan *features new initiatives* to take advantage of opportunities and/or protect current business.

_____ 6) If executed well, our strategy will *enhance our competitive position* in the future.

16.

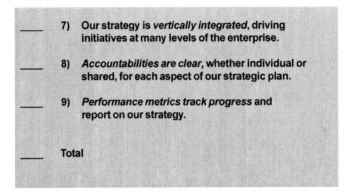

_____ 7) Our strategy is *vertically integrated*, driving initiatives at many levels of the enterprise.

_____ 8) *Accountabilities are clear*, whether individual or shared, for each aspect of our strategic plan.

_____ 9) *Performance metrics track progress* and report on our strategy.

_____ **Total**

Total your ratings. A total less than 18 suggests your strategy work could be much improved. If your total is between 10–27, there's solid value in your efforts, but also room for improvement. Totals over 27 suggest your strategy efforts are strongly coordinated and making the organizational impact you need.

Any items you didn't mark a 3 or 4 suggest possibilities for improvement.

Part 3

Strategy Concepts

- Three Ways to Compete

- Product Life Cycle

- Five Forces

- PIMS Research

- Competitive Advantage

- Sustainability

- Protective Barriers

- A New Look at Competitors

- Value Based Management

- Inventing the Future

Introduction to Strategy Concepts

In an earlier draft, we titled this section "strategy building blocks." That's because developing a strategy for your SBU, product group or functional area is something like a construction project. You can build an almost infinite variety of structures, yet there is a finite set of materials, building blocks, from which structures are made. In our work here, the building blocks are strategy concepts, ways of viewing and framing marketplace forces so we can manipulate them into new structures.

In this part of the book, we'll take several chapters to overview these building blocks. Not all of them will apply to your situation and, in fact, some will overlap with others in redundant or cross-cutting ways. Your job, of course, is to select for your use those building blocks, tools, and hard questions that apply best to your situation and can lead to the greatest insights.

Three Ways to Compete

"Those who pursue him hotly have many points of attack—
quality, design, service, and above all price . . ."
                                        –Clarence B. Randall

In crafting a strategy, you strive for a position that gives your business a sustainable competitive advantage. This is invariably a complex matter—involving your unique strengths, the structure of your industry, and the unique properties of your competitors and obstacles.

While your total business strategy may be quite complex, your competitive strategy, where the rubber meets the road with customers, is always constructed from building blocks which are, thankfully, not so complex. In fact, these building blocks have been followed by entrepreneurs for many years. What are they? In one of the clearest descriptions, Porter (1980) suggested three fundamental ways by which a firm or product group might outperform others. They are:

1) **Cost leadership**

2) **Differentiation**

3) **Focus**

Cost Leadership. Cost leadership means *overall* cost leadership—the total cost from product concept to customer delivery and, if possible, at every stage along the way. Any expensive links in the chain represent opportunities for

22.

others. It means constant pursuit of cost reductions, tight monitoring and control, optimum-scale facilities, and getting maximum output from every expenditure from sales and inbound logistics to production, outbound logistics and after sale services. Establishing a low-cost position *always* helps to protect a firm from its direct competitors because the firm can, if necessary, reduce prices until less efficient competitors must operate at zero (or negative) margins to maintain any share at all. Normally, overall cost leadership requires a relatively high market share and/or other advantages in raw materials, equipment, facilities, scale of operation, etc. A vigilant and aggressive competitor that has established the low cost position is always extremely difficult to dislodge.

> *"Not trying to learn and operate at the long-run least total cost imposes the risk of being forced out of business by a more astute and aggressive current or potential rival."*
> —D. Goldenberg

Long ago, Wal-Mart developed an integrated information and distribution system that yielded a modest, but highly reliable, cost advantage across its distribution system. Many credit the competitive advantages provided by this system with much of Wal-Mart's subsequent growth and success in a highly price-competitive market.

Differentiation. Differentiation is the second alternative building block. A firm makes its offering different from

23.

others in the minds of buyers, and thereby seeks to change the competitive game. It seeks to change the basis of competition from price-based commodity competition to unique goods/services at unique prices, offering benefits that the customer is willing to pay for and that are unique to its products/services. This approach normally requires strong research and development or other means of acquiring the unique product features, as well as an effective means of communicating the benefits to customers, often coupled with additional means of protecting the unique position (such as patents, trademarks, brand image, etc.). Such approaches are associated with higher-than-average margins, low to medium market share, and higher than average operating costs. Examples include all highly engineered products with high quality images, such as Porsche automobiles or Lennox heating/air conditioning systems. Other examples include those known for extraordinary service like Singapore Airlines, and products with secret or patented formulas like Classic Coke or Prozac.

Focus. The third building block involves focusing on a particular portion of a market and dominating it by better meeting its specific needs—offering a special range of products, lower costs, fuller service or providing some other advantage that can be applied across a certain market segment. Focus is often the method by which a new entrant gains a foothold in an established market. At the outset, a

24.

focus strategy always means a limited share of the total market. Japanese manufacturers gained footholds in the U.S. automobile market by focusing on the lower end of the new car market. Retailers such as Neiman Marcus, strip malls in exclusive neighborhoods, and small-town insurance agencies all focus on particular segments of markets and strive to provide what their segments need and appreciate.

> *"[Focus] positions emerge from three distinct sources. . . producing a subset of an industry's products or services. . . serving most or all the needs of a particular group of customers. . . [or] segmenting customers who are accessible in different ways. "* –Michael Porter

Each of the three building blocks represents a distinct way for an organization to approach its customers in the face of competition. You will find that every fully-developed strategy either represents one of these building blocks or a mix of two or more. For example, a "customer value" strategy combines differentiation and price—an attempt to offer the customer a better package of product, service, and price than others provide.

In addition to the three potentially successful options, there is a low-profit, failing option called "stuck in the middle." The greatest danger in strategic thinking lies not in choosing the wrong building blocks. All have proven workable. The greatest danger lies in choosing none or choosing such a haphazard mix that you construct not a fortress, but a field of rubble. "Stuck in the middle" leads to no advantage and a losing enterprise. Among retailers, Sears has been cited as "stuck in the middle" during a period of time when J.C. Penney and others, facing some of the same obstacles, selected and deployed workable strategies.

Since the first formulation of these competitive building blocks, others have elaborated on them and attempted to refine the concepts. Some suggested that all competitive strategies are, at bottom, a matter of *differentiation*—with everyone seeking to make their offerings differ from others in the market (Mintzberg, 1988). On this view, *price* is simply one possible distinction, the use of which will be advantageous to the low-cost producer. Four other types of differentiation are *image* (in the mind of the customer), product/service *design*, product/service *quality*, and product/service *support*. Some reserve a sixth option, *undifferentiation*, for situations in which there is no basis for differentiation or a copycat approach is pursued.

To complete this discussion, let's note how the concept of *functionalities* has recently been added to the debate. Asking what functions a good or service fulfills for the customer, and comparing equivalent functionalities rather than equivalent products or services, tends to change, enlarge and add new insights to our view of competitors and competition. Wired telephones, wireless telephones, computers, FedEx, Priority Mail, UPS, etc. can all be thought of as product/service offerings, but their true positions as actual and potential competitors becomes clearer when we think of their functional equivalencies in meeting market demands for immediate communications, document transfers, image with customers, etc.

What's the bottom line? First, over the years we have seen continued refinement in ideas about competitive strategy and how firms appeal to customers in vying for business. Second, despite continual refinement, the ways of distinguishing one offering from others are actually very few. At the level of directly competing for the customer's business, only a handful of strategy building blocks have been discovered.

Product Life Cycle

"Planning for change must be the ever-present concern of every single executive." —Jesse Werner

The idea of a life cycle—for individual products or whole industries—has become one of the most significant and compelling concepts in management.

How we recognize and manage our position within a life cycle is vital to profitability and, therefore, a crucial aspect of business strategy. This is particularly true in all high-volume, high-margin industries with frequent product/service introductions, short development lead times, and acute competition. For example, it is said in the semiconductor industry that the first firm to market a viable new product type reaps 80% all profits attributable to that type. And the pace is fast—from introduction to old age, product life cycles in the chip industry can be 18 months or less. Similar conditions hold in e-commerce, the fast-moving fashion industry and, to a greater or lesser degree, in your business.

What's a product life cycle and how does it impact our thinking about competitive strategy?

The Life Cycle. Most products and services go through a four-phase life cycle of introduction, growth, maturity, and decline. Whole companies, and entire industries, often follow this pattern as well. The shape of the curve is not always exactly the same, but it generally follows a pattern of very low demand at introduction, rising sales during a growth period, slower growth or level sales during maturity, and progressively lower sales during the decline phase.

THE PRODUCT LIFE CYCLE

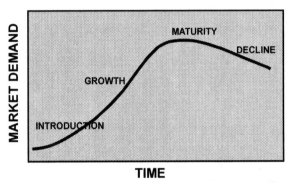

Introduction Stage—characterized by low sales, high unit costs, high prices, low profits and high risk as a small number of firms introduce a new product type and spend heavily to attract initial customers.

Growth Stage—characterized by rapidly increasing sales, higher profits, lower production costs, more competition, and decreasing prices.

Maturity Stage—characterized by high volumes, slower growth, leveling or declining profits, and declining prices.

29.

Decline Stage—characterized by high industry capacity, lower market demand, stable or falling prices, often declining sales and profits for individual firms.

While it may be dangerous to assume that all products go through this cycle in the same way, it's even more important to recognize that the cycle typically does apply. We see it in a very pure form in technology industries such as fiber optics, networking, and software. Imagine how these markets differ from those for soft drinks and air travel.

Life Cycle and Strategy. Should the life cycle affect our thinking about strategy? In a word, yes. It's critical to know what stage you're in and what stage your customers are in (if you are a supplier) as you think about your strategy for a product or business unit. If you have entered a new stage of the life cycle, your strategy may well have to be altered. This is tricky because we are sometimes too close to the action to recognize these patterns and because we are all reluctant to change what has worked in the past. The general pattern tying strategy to life cycle is characterized by a shift from differentiated products and high margins early in the life cycle to lower margins and price-based competition in mature and declining phases. Some firms are able to preserve product differentiation and competitive advantage well into mature markets (Coca-Cola in the U.S. soft drink market), but the pressure toward price competition remains.

At corporate levels, Coke and Pepsi may both be doing well in a mature domestic market, but a seesaw of price discounts constantly occurs at the retail end of the value chain.

The challenge to firms with mature products, markets, or industries is in devising ways to change the game. Various mechanisms can be deployed to alter the traditional shape of the life cycle curve—to increase the steepness of the growth portion, prolong the maturity, and/or slow the decline. In general, these are the same mechanisms used to protect an enterprise or product from competition (see Protective Barriers). You want to reshape the curve where you can, of course. But we must face the facts when a new phase of the life cycle has actually arrived and calls us to adjust the basis of competition to maintain earnings. You can readily see how the clothing industry copes by successively introducing new styles and the automobile industry by introducing new new classes of vehicles, such as the sport utility. Now style and fashion are even used in the maturing domestic market for home computers.

Those faced with maturing markets would do well to study how other firms and industries have responded to such conditions. Doing so, one finds that some have maintained fresh markets and products in maturing industries—it can be done.

Five Forces

"The harder the conflict, the more glorious the triumph."
                                        –Thomas Paine

At some point in crafting a strategy, we must go beyond all
the positive competitive advantages we expect to create and
delve into the dark side. What are the threats to our position,
our success, and our profitability? Where and from whom
might they arise?

Some of the threats you face come readily to mind. Others are
not so apparent and, therefore, it's a good practice to look for
them in a thorough and systematic way. One way to do this
is by using an analytic model of competition such as the Five
Forces Model (Porter, 1979). The five forces that bear on our
competitive position include two direct threats, the threat of
new entrants and the threat of substitutes. Two other forces
are economic ones, the bargaining power of suppliers and the
bargaining power of customers. The fifth force is the
competitive nature of our industry and the intensity of
rivalry that characterizes it.

Competitive Force #1—Potential New Competitors. This
threat is the one we naturally think of first, new competitors.
If we participate in a market that offers worthwhile earnings,
others will want to participate in that market as well.
Earnings attract competitors; you can count on it. Next to
death and taxes, it's the surest thing around—and about as
pleasant to contemplate. How many competitors are

FIVE COMPETITIVE FORCES

attracted and at what point additional competitors stop wanting to be in the market depends on the opportunities they perceive, the risks they perceive, their capabilities, and the barriers to entry.

Competitive Force #2—Substitutes. In most markets, traditional products/services can be threatened by the introduction of new or alternative ways to provide customers the same functionalities and benefits. Perhaps you can recall when soda bottles were sealed with a cork gasket under the cap. Cork suppliers were threatened, and eventually displaced, when plastic seals offered the same functionality with added benefits. Likewise, air travel has displaced much of what was formerly bus, rail and automobile travel.

Web commerce increasingly threatens conventional distribution chains, retail stores, libraries, catalogs, etc. by satisfying the same functional requirements. Outsourcing options threaten many corporate departments in Information Technology, Human Resources, Accounting, and other areas. In various ways, we all face the threat of substitutes.

> *"The sole producer of a specific product is not a monopolist; a true monopolist is the only producer of a good with no close substitutes."*
> –D. Goldenberg

Competitive Force #3—Supplier Bargaining Power. Suppliers have varying amounts of power over pricing, service, delivery and other terms of business. Their power is greater if the supply channel is dominated by only a few companies or if their product is unique. For example, companies operating at the forefront of chip technology, such as Intel and Texas Instruments, have relatively few direct competitors and sell into markets where they have many customers. Those who manufacture computers, cellphones and modems are many, but those who supply key components are few and, therefore, enjoy an added measure of bargaining power. Likewise, a supplier's bargaining power is higher if there are few substitute products, if the supplier can threaten vertical integration, or if suppliers are not dependant, in turn, on their customers for business in other areas.

34.

Under the opposite circumstances, it's a "buyer's market" and suppliers have correspondingly less bargaining power. Historically, various tactics and mechanisms have been applied to alter the power of suppliers or to change the game by interlocking suppliers and customers into partnership units. Around 1970, RCA vertically integrated its TV picture tube manufacturing by establishing a glass plant; their new business unit not only had a ready customer for all it could produce, but also improved the company's bargaining position with Corning and other glass suppliers.

Competitive Force #4—Customer Bargaining Power. Each firm has a certain amount of "pricing power" or ability to determine the price at which its transactions with customers will occur and, thereby, its profit margin. Customers also have a certain amount of bargaining power depending on their need for the product, alternative sources, etc. If you can establish a seller's market by offering a unique item for which the customer has a strong need, and no suitable substitutes or alternative sources, you will have considerable pricing power and the customer little bargaining power. This pricing power increases further if you have many customers or have less need than the customer does to make the transaction at a particular point in time. Examples of low customer bargaining power abound in fields ranging from artwork to health care. Customer bargaining power is highest for

35.

commodity items that are oversupplied, readily available from many providers, and for which numerous substitutes are available. A bumper crop of any agricultural product is a good example and, in consumer markets, much the same is true in food, appliances, automobiles, etc.

Competitive Force #5—Industry Rivalry. The degree of day-to-day rivalry, or jockeying for position, in a market varies with many factors; in general it is higher when there are many competitors, slow market growth, similar products, high fixed costs, perishable products, high exit barriers, or production capacity is comes in discrete steps.

> *"In business, the competition will bite you if you keep running; if you stand still, they will swallow you."*
> –William S. Knudson

Industry Growth. In rapidly growing industries that offer good growth opportunities for many providers, rivalry tends to be low; in mature or declining industries, it tends to be higher. If industry decline continues, consolidation sets in.

Industry Concentration. In general, more competitors of similar size in an industry leads to more intense competition, often on a price basis.

Diversity of Competition. The more diverse the strategies, resources, etc. of firms in an industry, the higher the degree of rivalry tends to be.

Corporate Strategy. Business units that are, or become, parts of large corporations may increase rivalry in their industries because of pressure from corporate.

Capital Intensity. High capital investment, especially in fixed plant and equipment, tends to keep firms eager for the volumes necessary to cover these costs. Rivalry further intensifies if growth slows and excess capacity develops.

Exit Barriers. High exit barriers sometimes make it more expensive to exit an undesirable market than to stay. High capital investment, noted earlier, is one such barrier. This is particularly true if the facilities and equipment are specialized and not readily adaptable to other uses. Other exit barriers may include contracts and agreements, government restrictions, focused expertise, inflexible distribution channels, and pride.

The five competitive forces jointly characterize much about the competitive environment you face. In your strategy work, the Five Forces Model is most likely to be useful as a roadmap in considering the threats to your business. Consider using this model if you do a threats assessment (see SWOT Analysis).

PIMS Research

"It is a capital mistake to theorize before one has data."
                                        –Arthur Conan Doyle

Despite all the theoretical and conceptual work on business strategy, there has been only one significant attempt to peer into the horse's mouth and actually count its teeth. PIMS stands for Profit Impact of Market Strategy—the only large scale study designed to measure the relationship between business strategy and business results.

The PIMS project was initiated by General Electric in the 1960s to study the factors behind the relative profitabilities of business units. It expanded and flourished at Harvard Business School in the early 1970s and was later adopted and managed by the non-profit Strategic Planning Institute.

The Data. From the beginning, this work has tried to take a fact-based approach to conclusions about business practices. The PIMS database contains a large amount of data on strategic business units (SBU's). For each of the thousands of SBU's in the database, values are recorded on hundreds of variables, including business type (consumer durables, raw materials, components, services, distribution, etc.), income and balance sheet figures, and data on quality, price, market share, markets, distribution, competitive tactics, etc.

Findings. The most general conclusions from the PIMS research have become common wisdom in business today.

PIMS FINDINGS

GENERAL CONCLUSIONS:

✔ It pays to be #1 or #2 in your market.

✔ Competing on quality is generally better than competing on price.

OTHER FINDINGS:

Investment. More fixed and working capital generally has a negative impact on percentage measures of profitability or net cash flow.

Productivity. High value added per employee is associated with higher profitability.

Market Share. High market share is associated with higher profits and cash flows. Low and high market shares are often associated with high ROIs. Middling market shares are often associated with lower ROIs.

Market Growth. A growing market generally means higher earnings, no change in margins, and lower cash flows.

Quality. Higher product/service quality is generally associated with better financial performance.

Innovation/differentiation. Investments in innovation, new and different products/services are generally associated with better financial performance if the firm is seen as a leader in the market, otherwise they have a negative effect.

Vertical Integration. In mature, stable markets vertical integration generally is associated with higher earnings; in changing, growing, or declining markets it generally is associated with lower earnings.

Strategic Initiatives. Efforts to change any of the above factors in a favorable direction is costly; it generally means lower profits and cash flows in the short term.

PIMS Caveats. The PIMS work reflects some of the most well founded conclusions in the business world and should, therefore, be taken seriously. At the same time, recognize that:

- These conclusions are based on historical data and circumstances may now differ.

- PIMS findings were developed across a wide range of SBU's and markets; your business and your markets may be exceptions.

- All PIMS findings are correlational, and we must take special care in thinking about which factor may be the cause and which the effect.

Despite its limitations, PIMS represents the best empirical data available on the business approaches that have succeeded in the past. PIMS member firms can contract, for a fee, to have original research conducted using the database.

Competitive Advantage

"When you win, nothing hurts." –Joe Namath

Competitive Advantage is a simple idea that stands at the heart of business strategy. It's the goal of all our efforts in strategy—to gain some distinction that allows us operate under more favorable terms than others do.

As a rule, economists have been among the most astute contributors on business strategy, and also the quickest to point out that many of our cherished schemes for gaining competitive advantage just don't hold water. Above all, they have asserted the terrible, but nevertheless correct, principle that the greatest opportunities for earnings will always attract additional competitors and offerings until the factors of earnings, risk, capital, know-how and other requirements are in balance with all other opportunities for earnings. The long-term pressure is always toward this state of equilibrium.

In the face of these forces, our never-ending search continues for distinctive capabilities, unique products/services, protectable market niches, and competitive advantages that are more-or-less sustainable. Likewise, a similar search continues for ways to mitigate the advantages of competitors and render them temporary rather than sustainable.

On the matter of sustainability, let's recognize first that there are only three ways the advantage of a distinctive capability can be lost, whether it is ours or a competitor's:

1)   The capability erodes.

2)   Others imitate and the capability is no longer distinctive.

3)   The market changes so that the distinctive capability is no longer an advantage.

Erosion of Capability. It's entirely possible for a business to simply let its distinctive advantage wither away. Most don't of course, but it does happen. For example, others might attract away your most talented designers, engineers, or researchers until your product development capability becomes second rate. Or, excessive striving for operational efficiency might result in discarding the very qualities that set you apart in the market. As someone said, "You can continue taking little bits of cheese off the pizza until there aren't any customers left." Or, one might neglect polishing the brand image until it no longer commands value in the marketplace.

Imitation. Loss of a competitive advantage most commonly results from competitors copying your success. Partially or wholly, legally or illegally, in truth or only in the minds of customers, most product/service distinctions can be copied or somehow mitigated. In some markets, the first to enter with a new product type reaps the major portion of the earnings; in others, copycat strategies can bring significant earnings while avoiding the expense of innovation and the risk of failed experiments.

Competitors can also imitate processes and operating efficiencies. From 1980 to the present, companies have taken a wide range of initiatives to improve their competitive positions in their industries and in the world economy. Faster–Better–Cheaper, Outsourcing, Process Management, Activity Based Costing, Performance Management and similar terms have been repeated over and over in strategic objectives and goals.

"No man ever yet became great by imitation."
–Samuel Johnson

As noted earlier, these initiatives succeeded and helped U.S. corporations become far more successful in the world economy than in the early 1980's—leaner, more agile, and more tuned to customers than ever before. But while some called these initiatives strategic, they did not lead to lasting competitive advantages. Why? Because everyone else followed the same path! Those who first focused on the customer, slimmed down, became more agile, and took out excess costs saw immediate gains, but others caught up all too soon by following their lead.

Market Changes. As markets change, the basis of competition changes and, with it, the factors that produce competitive advantage. In one example, automatic washers were a popular consumer item in Europe during the 1950's. Leading manufacturers built market share through long production runs and low prices. As incomes rose and consumers became a little less price sensitive, the basis of competition shifted from price to machine design and product distribution networks. The most profitable segments of the market no longer matched the distinctive capabilities of the early leaders. Much the same shift has occurred in certain automobile markets. Some manufacturers have adapted well to the new market opportunities (e. g., Toyota's introduction of the Lexus line) but most have been less successful competing on this new high ground (Nissan, Honda, and most U.S. makers). In another example, IBM's distinctive capability in mainframe computers remained intact during a time when much of the market shifted away toward distributed processing via desktop PCs.

So, where does this leave us? How's a firm to gain, and sustain, competitive advantage? There are two answers: find the advantages that *are* sustainable and/or deploy protective barriers. We take up these matters next.

Sustainability

"Corporate success rests on distinctive capabilities—on those characteristics of an organization that others cannot easily replicate, even when they have seen what they are and have observed the added value that others create through them."
            –John Kay

Four sources of competitive advantage have been identified that are, in principle, sustainable. They are *architecture, reputation, innovation,* and *strategic assets.* In actual practice, realizing a sustainable competitive advantage from any of the four calls for constant investment, effort, and vigilance.

Architecture. Appropriate architecture allows a firm to do unique things that can be translated into competitive advantage and, with effort, sustained. One example is Wal-Mart's inventory and product distribution structure. Years ago, this giant retailer invested in an architecture that tightly knit together its supply chain all the way from vendors to store shelves and allowed rapid, almost-real-time restocking with minimum inventories and minimum total cost. Their competitive advantage will be sustained until others somehow replicate this system or improve upon it.

Another kind of architecture allows a firm to generate a string of innovations. Not just a single flash in the pan, but innovation after innovation. That's not luck. Successive innovations come from an investment policy, structure, and culture—an architecture that brings forth innovations.

3M and Hewlett-Packard are among the best-known for this capability.

Yet another kind of architecture enables a firm to quickly and effectively convert new technologies into successful products. Who invented color TV and the CCD imaging devices at the heart of camcorders? RCA. Who makes all the money on them today? Not RCA. It's those who have architectures and capabilities tuned to product development and consumer marketing. During the last half of the 20th century, several Japanese firms have been acknowledged as leaders in the architectures required for this kind of competitive advantage.

Reputation. Reputation, or brand image in consumer markets, is another source of sustainable competitive advantage, and again one that requires careful nurturing and vigilance. Coca-Cola nurtures a brand image of staggering worldwide value, yet one that can receive billion-dollar blows by any error in testing, manufacturing process, water quality, etc. Many car makers could weather a safety-related recall on half a million vehicles without too much damage to their reputations, but not Mercedes or Volvo. So long as they are protected and enhanced, the reputations of these firms— and others like Sony, Lennox and many more—will bring continuing advantages in selling goods and services.

Innovation. As with all sources of sustainable competitive advantage, innovation calls for continual investment, effort, and vigilance to realize. As noted earlier, 3M and Hewlett-Packard are among those best known for using innovation as a source of sustainable competitive advantage. Even if a particular innovation is copied by competitors, the innovator is always in the market first and had the opportunity to build both product loyalty and market share. Nowhere is this more true than in semiconductor chips and pharmaceutical products.

> *"Sooner or later innovation radically changes the game. Innovation is the only source of economic profits aside from luck."* –D. Goldenberg

Realizing a sustainable competitive advantage from innovation calls for much more than a strong research department. The problems are several. At the front end, the work of innovation is costly and the results uncertain; the work itself is hard to manage, calls for special skills, and is notoriously resistant to systematic management. At the back end, successful outcomes are difficult to protect, defend, and convert into sustained earnings.

The latter point refers to the problem of "appropriability"—that is, ensuring that the results are profitable to you and only to you. Among the mechanisms for ensuring appropriability are: *patents, licenses, and legal restrictions; secrecy;* and *strategic combinations.*

48.

Patents and legal restrictions are obvious and known to work pretty well in some industries, such as pharmaceuticals, and less well in others.

Secrecy is, on average, not well regarded as a pathway to sustainable competitive advantage. In addition to the threats of reverse engineering and outright theft, our relatively open society encourages and values the sharing of professional knowledge and best practices. Without realizing it, professionals are sometimes balancing their own career interests with those of the firm when they participate in benchmarking studies, give papers at professional conferences, etc. While it's true that many firms give away information too freely, those who scoff at the effectiveness of secrecy policies should try to pry even the smallest operational detail from a business unit at Procter and Gamble.

By all odds, the most effective way of using innovation involves combining it with another strategic capability, asset, or tactic. Sony combines innovation with brand image in personal listening devices; banks combine innovation with distribution or processing prowess when they offer new, non-traditional financial services; test equipment firms combine software innovations with proprietary hardware.

Strategic Assets. The fourth source of sustainable competitive advantage, and one of the most effective, is the control of strategic assets. Those who own or control access to the assets essential to certain goods and services will enjoy a competitive advantage for as long as they can maintain control and the assets remain essential. The most obvious examples are in natural resources, where paper companies control vast forest reserves, petroleum companies control vast oil reserves, and cable companies and regional telephone companies control vast networks of cable and copper hookups to homes and businesses. Similar, and less obvious, phenomena occur in many industries; you can probably see how some operate in your industry.

A general clue in the search for sustainable advantages is to elevate your thought process up one level of abstraction or generality. For example:

- While a single innovation generally does not result in a sustainable advantage, the capability to generate successive innovations may be sustainable.

- While a single natural resource holding may not bring a permanent competitive advantage, the capability of finding and acquiring such resources may be sustainable.

What are the present competitive advantages enjoyed by various firms in your markets? Are they sustainable? Would they be sustainable if we moved the question up one level of generality?

Protective Barriers

"The best armor is to keep out of range."
                                   –Italian Proverb

The most basic model of competition is the sale of a commodity product in a large market with many suppliers and many customers. Other things being equal, these situations quickly resolve to pure price competition, vigorous jockeying, and narrow margins. In this chapter we will explore the "other things being equal" part of the equation— the various forces and factors that change the simple model toward other bases of competition and, often, toward higher margins. Your earnings depend on knowing and using these factors.

In every market, certain factors operate to reduce the number of competitors or change the basis on which firms compete with one another. Economists call these "barriers," "protective barriers," or "barriers to entry." These barriers mix and match to produce an almost infinite variety of competitive subtleties across markets and market segments.

Barriers exist for many reasons. Some are economic, some are strategic, some technological, some legal, and some are a function of the capabilities of the enterprise. They may be classified as on the following page.

TYPES OF PROTECTIVE BARRIERS

- Product/service differentiation
- Technological, legal, and knowledge barriers
- Economic barriers
  - Capital Requirements
  - Economies of Scale
- Strategic barriers
  - Supply Limitations
  - Retaliation Threats
  - Distribution Access

Consider which of these barriers now apply in your competitive situation and which ones may offer the best opportunities for further deployment in the future.

Product/Service Differentiation. As noted earlier, a product/service offering that is unique and appreciated by loyal customers presents a formidable barrier to new competitors. Aspiring competitors often find getting even a small market share enormously expensive and a significant share simply unattainable. Imagine trying to compete with Coca-Cola in its main product line. Cosmetics, fashion designers, certain automobiles, brewers, and many others also enjoy such advantages. The source of the "differentness" that appeals to customers can be in the product itself, or any aspect of it from customization to delivery, individual attention, service and information, etc. so long as it is clearly different in the minds of buyers.

53.

Technological, Legal, and Knowledge Barriers. This large class of protective barriers includes the famous "learning curve" or "experience curve." The accumulated history of a firm in developing, producing, and marketing a particular type of product gives it advantages over insurgents in driving down costs, deploying best practices, and averting errors as successive generations of products are developed. Just imagine entering the market for digital signal processing chips to compete with an established leader like Texas Instruments. The most astute such firms have applied process management to their entire value chains from product concept to market availability—minimizing cycle times and error rates and maximizing throughputs.

> *"Experience is what enables you to recognize a mistake when you make it again."*
> –Earl Wilson

In addition to the unique capabilities represented by their experience curves, leading firms usually also have proprietary technologies that are protected by patents and are, therefore, unavailable to new entrants.

Beyond the technological and legal barriers they enjoy, some firms have also become adept in creating, sharing, and putting new knowledge to work. Established mechanisms allow them to store and access their wealth of experience, putting this know how to use throughout their enterprises.

Economic Barriers.

1)   Capital requirements. Some markets and products require vast sums of capital from every player that participates. The airline industry offers a good example. While a bright idea and and a little office space may suffice to start a dot-com enterprise, airlines are different. Even starting small means starting big. The cost of aircraft, equipment, facilities, salaries, customer credit, inventory, advertising, etc. mean that such businesses—by their nature—require vast sums of capital and, thereby, present barriers to entry for new competitors. In other situations, established enterprises may have infrastructures that cannot be reasonably duplicated in the current economy. Their sunk costs, fully depreciated equipment, etc. give them advantages in operating costs that cannot be overcome and that could, if necessary, be translated into aggressive pricing practices that would prevent an insurgent from ever gaining a significant market share.

2)   Economies of scale. Even when they can meet the capital requirements to enter a market, aspiring competitors are commonly faced with enormous disadvantages of scale. They may develop and bring to market a new airline, automobile or mainframe computer, but remain at an extreme cost disadvantage to those already holding large positions in the market. Research, marketing, production,

55.

service and advertising all cost disproportionately more at small volumes. A new airline may get the gates it needs and establish a few routes, but will almost surely have the disadvantage of small scale when it comes to aircraft maintenance and all corporate functional departments.

Strategic Barriers. Some of the most interesting protective barriers are strategic in nature—supply limitations, distribution access, and retaliation threats. Established firms can sometimes set agreements with suppliers that give them priority or exclusive access, perhaps in exchange for favorable terms on pricing, delivery, or an agreement to not vertically integrate, effectively shutting out new entrants. For example, dominant retailers are sometimes positioned to forge agreements with suppliers that not only give them favorable pricing, but specify increasingly favorable terms in the future. Some retailers, such as Wal-Mart, require such terms in exchange for the extreme volumes and distribution they offer. From the supplier's point of view, such arrangements may also appear strategically favorable if they result in exclusive access to the most favored channel of distribution.

Retaliation can also be threatened, explicitly or implicitly, by an established firm to discourage additional competition. Potential entrants can sometimes check the historical record to see what has happened before. For example, imagine that a major software vendor were to consider offering a new web browser or an ultra-reliable PC operating system. Existing players have not only offered fierce competition to such entrants in the past, but are said to have brought reprisals in other areas, such as the development of new products to compete in the entrant's other markets. For an even more graphic example, consider what happens when criminal gangs consider expanding into new products or geographic territories.

The competitive factors we've examined in this chapter are described by economists as "barriers to entry" or "barriers to competition." True, they do limit competition from the consumer's perspective. From the perspective of firms participating in these markets, however, barriers do not eliminate competition; they change the basis on which competition occurs. You might even think of these barriers as the levers and handles which help you determine the basis on which competition will be played out. For example, the phamaceutical firm that uses the barrier of patent protection for a group of compounds has not eliminated competition, but shifted its basis for competition from retail price competition in a commodity market to competition based on research, patent registration, and marketing.

New Look at Competitors

"There is no resting place for an enterprise in a competitive economy." —Alfred P. Sloan

Since strategy is, by and large, about prevailing over competitors and obstacles, let's say a few words about who your competitors are.

Of course, if you've been in business any length of time, you know who your competitors are. Traditionally, we've considered competitors to be those who make alternative offerings in our markets. These direct competitors vie for the same sales to the same customers, on more or less the same product or service. Or they provide the same functionalities or benefits through other products/services. They are the competitors you think of first, who are always there, and are sometimes the cause of sleepless nights.

Another group, your potential competitors, normally come from two sources—those who have access to your customers but do not offer comparable products/services, and those who have the means to produce comparable products/services but are not now doing so. Potential competitors—who they are, how ready they are to enter our markets, and what we can do to prevent them from competing effectively—are an important aspect of your strategic thinking.

So we have direct competitors and potential competitors. Is that all? No, unfortunately. In our work, a third type of competitor has become apparent—the indirect competitor.

One kind of indirect competitor sells to our customers but does not offer comparable products/services. We sell kitchen appliances and they provide lawn sprinklers. Why are they competitors? Because they vie for the same share of the customer's finite resources. Since customers cannot buy everything, nor do they have time to use all the goods and services offered, somewhere there's a *crunch*. This is most easily seen in consumer markets. Software games, clothing, and movies are all indirect competitors for the money of young people. Perhaps you find that work, family activities, gardening, church and community service are all indirect competitors for your time. Indirect competitors do not vie on equivalent goods and services; they simply offer mutually exclusive uses for the same resource, usually *money* or *time*. In the final analysis, our case for getting the customer's business must be sufficiently compelling versus our indirect competitors that we get the business. Consider for a moment how such indirect competitors may be affecting your business and industry.

A second type of indirect competitor is even more remote, not addressing your customers in any way. While we may be thankful that we do not compete in some of today's hottest

59.

industries, that gratitude can quickly vanish when we enter the capital markets and compete with them for funds, or simply face the high investor expectations left in their wake. Indirect competitors affect the prices we pay and the access we have to capital, raw materials, distribution, and—perhaps most of all—talent. Intel, Microsoft, and Silicon Valley may not be competing for your customers, but they are very effective indirect competitors if you require top-level software engineers. Indirect competitors are forcing all of us to look and act like growth companies.

What can we conclude from all this? First, we face more competitors than we usually think. Second, we need strategies that take all competitors into account—lest we develop a winning approach to gain sales from our current direct competitors, but cannot counter a potential competitor or a deadly indirect competitor.

TYPES OF COMPETITORS

✔ Direct Competitors—those who offer same functionalities or benefits to same customers.

✔ Potential Competitors—those who could enter market and become direct competitors.

✔ Indirect Competitors 1—those who vie for same resources of customers, usually money or time.

✔ Indirect Competitors 2—those who vie for key inputs, or set performance expectations in market.

Value Based Management

"First, create customer value, without which there can be no shareholder value."   –George S. Day

In recent years, an important theme in enterprise management has been Value Based Management. It asserts that the purpose of every organization is to create value. Creating value is, likewise, also the purpose of every line of business, every department, and every individual in an organization. Cash money is the most widely recognized and accepted form of such value but other, equally valid, forms also exist. Consider an organization where the mission is to assure the safety of our nuclear stockpile and reduce the risk of nuclear accidents. Is value being created in the form of safety and security? Certainly. Value Based Management suggests there are many forms of tangible and intangible value, each legitimate if it is prized by customers and desired in the market. Some types of value can be readily converted to dollar equivalents, some cannot.

Value Based Management calls for leaders at every level to know what kind of value their organizations, departments, and individuals are creating. To gauge success, we must be able to measure or somehow assess how much of each kind of value is being created. To improve performance, leaders must align the types of value being created with those prized in the market, increase them, and tune efforts toward these types of value and away from non-value activities.

Thus, Value Based Management is an integrated approach to rationalizing an organization, tuning every aspect of it toward a market. It calls for asking and constantly re-asking certain questions:

KEY QUESTIONS FOR VALUE BASED MANAGEMENT

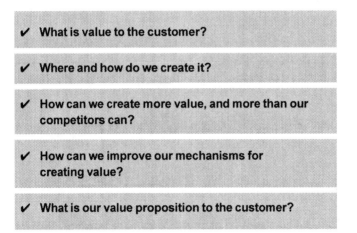

✔ **What is value to the customer?**

✔ **Where and how do we create it?**

✔ **How can we create more value, and more than our competitors can?**

✔ **How can we improve our mechanisms for creating value?**

✔ **What is our value proposition to the customer?**

To help answer these questions, consider applying the methodology of Value Chain Analysis. This analysis begins with the types of value being delivered to the customer and works backward through the organization to analyze where and how these types of value are created. More detailed analyses allow every part of the

63.

organization to determine how its activities contribute to the output value of the larger organization and how they may be better tuned to do so. Actions are commonly taken to shorten the value chain, optimize the value-adding activities it contains, and reduce or eliminate non-value-adding activities where possible (see Value Chain Analysis).

Value Based Management benefits strategic thought primarily by forcing an external focus and directing attention toward customer value, benefits and functionalities. Because it begins with present-day markets and customers, Value Based Management is stronger as a strategy tool when complemented by mechanisms that add a forward-looking perspective (see End User Scenarios).

Inventing the Future

"The best way to predict the future is to create it."
–Jason Kaufmann

A strategic perspective we call Inventing the Future begins from the same customer-focused foundation as Value Based Management. However, it emphasizes leading the customer into the future rather than responding to the customer's presently articulated needs and values.

On this view, there are three kinds of businesses. One focuses inwardly on its products and technologies, developing successive offerings it hopes will sell to customers. Traditional banks, fashion, and entertainment businesses are good examples. The second kind of business is customer focused, paying close attention to what customers say and striving to provide the features and benefits they want. Many manufacturing and service

THREE TYPES OF COMPANIES

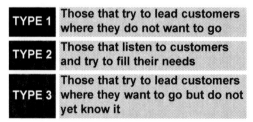

TYPE 1	Those that try to lead customers where they do not want to go
TYPE 2	Those that listen to customers and try to fill their needs
TYPE 3	Those that try to lead customers where they want to go but do not yet know it

companies operate this way. The third kind of business is also customer focused, but tries to provide what customers will want in the future—leading the market rather than responding to it. These businesses, often in high-tech industries, take the position that customers do not know what is technically possible and must, therefore, be led into the future by those who do know. This third approach is called by some "creating the future" or creating new "competitive space" (Hamel and Prahalad, 1994).

"Our [Sony's] plan is to lead the public with new products rather than ask them what kind of products they want."
–Akio Morita

How do leading companies invent the future?

1) They begin by studying how customers live, rather than asking what they want.

2) They search out and test new benefits that might apply to certain customer lifestyles.

3) They become first to build the core competencies and capabilities necessary to deliver the new benefits.

4) They establish coalitions and partnerships that set technical standards and industry rules.

5) They build on existing franchises to sell the new benefits.

As an example of the latter point, Sony has a dominant position in personal entertainment and can be expected to build out this franchise in the future.

67.

A firm's most valuable assets for inventing the future include its core competencies, its franchise with customers, its intellectual property, its people and talent, its image and reputation, its ability to learn how to contribute value, and its ability to erect competitive barriers such as industry standards. A package of such assets, when they properly interrelate, is called a "strategic architecture" and constitutes a powerful competitive weapon.

From the perspective of inventing the future, traditional strategic planning is seen as too incremental, analytic and formula driven. Here's a summary of the differences:

	Focus of Traditional Planning	Focus of Inventing the Future
Goal	Incremental improvement in mkt share/position	Rewrite rules, create new competitive space
Planning Process	Begin from current industry structure and markets	Begin from discontinuities, abrupt changes, and org competencies
	Analyze markets, value chain, costs & competitors	Search new functionalities and delivery methods
	Plan=primarily spreading resources among projects	Plan=gain competencies, exploit opportunities, migration path
Test for	Fit of resources and plans	Significance of opportunities/timeliness
Unit of Analysis . .	SBU or product group	Whole corporation

Inventing the future is an important concept in strategy. Though it may apply widely, its popularity so far has been greatest in high tech organizations where competition is keen and new products, new functionalities, and new delivery mechanisms are being rapidly developed.

What conclusions should we draw here?

1) Most organizations should give more time and attention to creating new competitive space, particularly those in maturing industries.

2) Beginning with customer functionalities leads to powerful new insights that differ from those derived from products, markets, and industries.

3) New competitive space can be dominated by those who plan ahead to build organizational competencies, set new technical standards, and develop advantageous migration paths.

4) There is risk involved in creating new competitive space. A firm might invest significant sums and realize few returns or find itself out in left field.

5) To compete in the most favorable arenas, we must learn to look deeply and creatively into the future, in a way that combines customer and emerging technologies. We should use the best strategy tools available for this (see End User Scenarios) and develop additional ones.

69.

Part 4

Tools and Methods

- SWOT Analysis

- Value Chain Analysis

- Basis of Competition Analysis

- Scenario Mapping

- End User Scenarios

Introduction to Tools

So far, we've reviewed most of the significant concepts and building blocks of strategy. Soon we will be looking into the actual work of crafting strategy. Before that, however, there's one more important topic—we call it Tools and Methods.

In this section you'll find tools designed for understanding, organizing, and presenting the strategic environment faced by your organization. Carefully done, such strategic analyses form a background of common understanding for the important decisions faced by your organization. Because this background influences the decisions taken, the very best analyses for your situation will be those that are carefully selected and adapted for your circumstances. Not all the following will fit your organization, but several are likely to be good starting points for a custom design.

SWOT Analysis

"Know the enemy and know yourself; in a hundred battles you will not be in peril."   –Sun Tzu

One of the earliest tools for situation assessment in strategy has also turned out to be one of the most enduring: SWOT Analysis. The name stands for strengths, weaknesses, opportunities, and threats. Though sometimes presented in different forms, this analysis has remained at the heart of many strategic planning systems over the years. When new models are offered, they often turn out to be sub-analyses that elaborate on one part or another of the traditional SWOT Analysis.

SWOT ANALYSIS

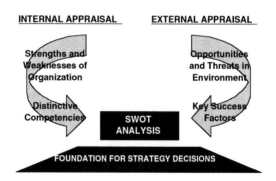

The strengths and weaknesses portion of the SWOT Analysis addresses *internal* factors and includes the organization's distinctive competencies, technologies, processes, distribution systems, design and development, its

vulnerabilities, and other internal factors that enhance or detract from the strength of its position in a given market. Anytime we call factors strengths and weaknesses, we raise the question "Compared to what?" The answer, of course, has to be "compared to rivals and potential rivals in the market." We like to list your strengths and weakness side by side with primary competitors.

The Opportunities and Threats portion of the SWOT Analysis addresses factors *external* to the enterprise, including opportunities to strengthen position vs. rivals and/or shift to a new group of rivals. For example, by adding features to its offering, the enterprise may be able to move into a new peer group offering specialized products. The threats facing a firm might include the possibility of new rivals entering its markets, the possibility of losing bargaining power with suppliers or customers, or increased competition from substitute products/services. See the Five Forces chapter for a model useful in conducting and presenting the Opportunities and Threats portion of a SWOT Analysis.

Conducting a SWOT Analysis. The right mix of talents and a useful analysis model are two of the important ingredients in conducting your SWOT Analysis.

Talents. Here's a checklist of talents for a successful SWOT Analysis. The work calls for a team that brings:

- ✔ Deep knowledge of the enterprise, industry, customers, and competitors.

- ✔ Strong analytic abilities.

- ✔ An unbiased outlook.

- ✔ Ability to present unpopular views if necessary.

Because the work benefits from exploring and cross-checking different views, SWOT Analyses are best conducted by teams with carefully chosen members. Outside coaches or facilitators are frequently helpful.

Analysis Model. Your SWOT Analysis will also benefit from a guiding model. Random thinking and brainstorming tend toward inefficient and incomplete results. Your model should establish an appropriate breadth of analysis for the work and suggest where to look for SWOT's. On breadth, the chief question is how many organizations to include in the analysis. Your own enterprise or product line is the focus, but it's important to include one, two, or more of your primary competitors and perhaps your whole industry taken collectively. On where to look for SWOT's, you'll find that a set of thought guides will make the search more efficient and orderly. The value chain for your organization is often a useful guide, as is the Five Forces model, or a custom set of factors chosen from such items as: products, research and development, financial resources, operating costs, dealer/distribution, marketing/sales, technology, etc.

A useful analytic method is to draw a matrix that has columns for your firm and several competitors. Rows in the matrix contain the "where to look" factors determined above. Such a matrix can be used to guide the analysis as you consider and document the strengths, weaknesses, opportunities and threats that apply for each cell. Be sure to include not just the present state of affairs, but how you expect competitors to behave in the future and the SWOT's that will apply.

Value Chain Analysis

Because Value Based Management was outlined earlier, we need not review it further here. Let us, however, say a little more about Value Chain Analysis as a tool for implementing this approach and preparing for strategy deliberations.

Value Chain Analysis simply applies the ideas of process management at a level where we can see how value is created for customers—usually the SBU level or the product/service level. In designing your Value Chain Analyses, the breadth and level of detail you choose to engage will be key factors.

Breadth. All proper Value Chain Analyses begin with the nature of the value being provided to the customer or consumer. There is no other legitimate foundation. From this starting point, the broadest analyses span backward to the original product/service concept or even further to the capability that enables the organization to envision such benefits.

Depth. Value Chain Analyses typically identify the stages of value creation at very high levels (see following figure). Such a generic approach may suffice for your organization, but most will want to conduct more detailed examinations that look deeper into each major segment of the chain.

TYPICAL SBU VALUE CHAIN

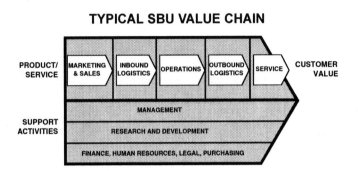

Of course, the value chain for your particular product or service may or may not follow the categories and exact sequence of a typical chain. If your analysis is more detailed, the chain leading to customer value will contain more links and more fine-grained descriptions of the activities by which value is created at each stage.

What does all this mean to your strategy? To tie the analysis to your strategy, you will want to consider the value chain from at least three points of view: *creating value*, *reducing cost*, and *disintermediation*.

Creating Value. To look for strategically important information in your Value Chain Analysis, you'll want to consider each link and ask the most penetrating questions possible about how value, as defined by the customer, is created at this stage or added by the activities at this stage. This typically leads to more detailed analyses of the links in the value chain and the

79.

identification of certain activities critical to producing what the customer values. The examination and documentation of how these activities might create more value for the same or less cost, or value that exceeds the cost of producing it, result in important inputs for your strategy deliberations.

Reducing Cost. Examining your value chain from the cost reduction perspective is much like examining it from the value creation perspective, except that the focus is on questions of how similar value might be produced at less cost by each value-adding activity. Or how non-value-adding activities can be accomplished at less cost or eliminated entirely. Again documenting these options provides inputs useful in strategy deliberations.

Disintermediation. The third way Value Chain Analysis bears on strategy can lead to the most dramatic changes in your business. Disintermediation refers to shortening the value chain and finding more direct ways to deliver the desired value to the customer. Many firms are succeeding in eliminating jobbers, wholesalers, brokers, and other "middlemen" in the inbound and outbound segments of their value chains. By their logic, the ideal value chain would have one step linking the product concept to the experience of value or benefit by the customer. While such an ideal is seldom achievable, creative solutions and new technologies are making it possible to come ever closer. All three perspectives on your value chain—value added, cost reduction, and disintermediation—are options that can yield extremely useful inputs for your strategy deliberations.

Basis of Competition Analysis

The basis on which you compete is another crucial starting point for developing or revising strategy.

We like to use a Basis of Competition Analysis to add a strong real-world perspective to your strategy deliberations. Your organization certainly has a theory or philosophy of how it competes, but how well does this concept play out in everyday competition? How well does it describe the everyday decisions made by real people in your markets? In short, is your real day-to-day basis for competition what your strategy says it is?

Goal of the Analysis. For a given market, the Basis of Competition Analysis attempts to answer three simple questions:

1) **Where does competition occur?**

2) **Who decides the purchase?**

3) **What is the decision based upon?**

While simple, immediate answers to these questions are sometimes possible, the most useful answers for your strategy deliberations are likely to involve sub-issues that can involve more research.

Where Does Competition Occur? Where are your points of competition? At what places and times is your offering compared to others? Where and when are decisions made about your product or key impressions formed that later determine decisions? Does this occur in a dealer's showroom, a Board Meeting, before a computer screen, during a Super Bowl ad, in a family discussion, in the mind of a purchasing agent, or exactly where? How many buys are based on impulse and how many on careful analysis, advice and information? Whose advice and information? The answers begin to tell where your case must be effectively presented to the customer.

Who Decides the Purchase? That is, who makes the decision to choose your offering or your competitor's offering? Who determines the outcome? Is it a purchasing agent, a family, a board of directors, a dealer or distributor, a child? McDonald's, for example, knows that children are very influential in determining which fast food restaurants families choose. You may find several decision makers and several influencers, particularly if you are considering more than one market or customer group.

What is the Decision Based Upon? Here's the heart of the matter. On what basis does the deciding person choose an offering? What functionalities are sought? What musts and wants are involved? What appeals to the decision maker at

83.

the time the decision is made? Is there one overwhelming decision factor, or many contributing factors? Some organizations spend considerable research dollars to have accurate, up to date answers to these key questions. And some don't. Many find that the answers are not as obvious as they seem at first and/or that they may change over time. They also find that a completely rational analysis is seldom the full answer, because buying decisions occur in the minds of customers and are based on facts and values as they are perceived—not as they are to a rational observer.

Finding the Answers. Finding valid answers calls for research designed around your unique circumstances and markets. In most cases, a properly designed research effort will rely on three sources of information: internal knowledge, customers, and transactions.

Internal Knowledge. First, you'll want to accumulate the knowledge and wisdom resident in your organization—particularly from key executives and front line salespersons. Data from these sources will be immensely valuable, yet must be used with caution as these inputs can be out of date or more swayed by what the basis of competition is supposed to be than by what it is.

Customers. The second source of data is customers. Formal or informal, brief or extensive, direct customer research is a crucial input to your Basis of Competition Analysis. For the actual data, it's sometimes possible to rely on ongoing customer research, either by using existing data or adding new components to customer studies.

Transactions. Transaction research is our third input to a Basis of Competition Analysis. It is often the most important source of data as it can verify, elaborate and validate the other sources of data in a more objective way; transaction data will either confirm the common view of how the organization competes for sales or surprise people greatly.

Transaction research involves selecting a valid sample of customer sales (by random sampling or, more commonly, stratified random sampling) and checking the actual basis on which competition occurred in those transactions. Naturally, the details of such an effort will depend on the nature of your business and such an effort will not be suitable in all industries. We find that the results, however, can be quite enlightening—sometimes revealing that the actual basis of competition differs markedly from what people think, or that it varies greatly with time and place.

For example, imagine you've worked long and hard to develop a highly engineered product, differentiated from competitors by superior performance. Production costs are high, but product performance justifies a premium price and good margins. Or so you believe. Suppose your field sales people are compensated for reaching various sales totals by time periods. In such cases, it's not uncommon to learn from transaction data that certain circumstances (highly contested sales situations, approaching monthly deadlines, etc.) result in a fair percentage of low-margin, price-based transactions that deviate from the high value, high margin approach defined as the basis of competition in the business strategy. This may be a fact of life in your industry, but it's also a significant discontinuity in your strategy deployment and key background information for your future strategy. You may wish to do a more comprehensive modeling of transactions that shows what proportion of sales, at what times and places, actually follow your prescribed business strategy and what proportion follow various alternative bases of competition.

Valuable Preparation. In a Basis of Competition Analysis, we set out with three questions in mind: Where does competition occur, who decides the purchase, and what is the decision based upon? The answers to these three questions say a lot about how you actually compete in today's market. Does this understanding of competition square with your strategy? Is this basis favorable to you and your enterprise capabilities, or not? In what ways? Will the present situation hold in the future, or is it likely to change? Should you attempt to alter the basis of competition? What would a more favorable situation look like?

A Basis of Competition Analysis, like the other tools suggested here as starting points, can be a key input to your strategy deliberations. It does not suit every situation, but for many SBU's and product groups, it's invaluable.

Scenario Mapping

"Let us not go over the old ground, let us rather prepare for what is to come." —Cicero

Are you preparing for an uncertain future? Scenario mapping is a tool specifically developed to help you peer into a dimly-lit future; it's a tool that deserves more use today.

One reason scenario mapping deserves more use is the change we see all around us. Scenarios help in pulling facts together and making sense of change and complexity. Scenario mapping can also help open thinking in your organization, challenge your assumptions, and prepare for the possibility of new competitive rules and a different future than you might predict from the past. Scenario mapping is your best tool for this kind of thinking.

In Scenario Mapping you catalog the issues, trends and facts about your organization's future that are most certain, as well as those that are less certain, and use them to assemble logically consistent pictures of how the future might unfold. The two keys to success in scenario mapping are choosing the right variables and facts as your base and employing a powerful, but realistic, imagination.

Scenario mapping always means creating multiple pictures of the future. Part of its value comes in shaking up our normal ideas that routinely picture only one likely future. A set of scenarios describes internal and external environments that vary in likelihood. Each suggests decisions and actions required now to prepare for a particular future and, by choosing carefully, you may be able to prepare for several possible futures. Scenarios not only help in this preparation, they also alert and sensitize us to the right clues so that we can more quickly recognize the true scenario as it unfolds and respond accordingly.

> *"An effective scenario almost always changes behavior."*
> –Peter Schwartz

For a simplified example of how scenarios work, consider the U.S. stock market in the late 1990s. Two factors widely thought to be involved in its rise were:

✔ The flow of foreign investment, which varies with the strength of local economies abroad.

✔ The positive public perception in the U.S. of the market as an investment vehicle.

In the late 1990's, both factors were unusually positive. Based on these two relevant variables, we can construct four scenarios for the few years following this period:

1) Foreign economies recover slowly, so foreign funds continue to flow into U.S. markets *and* public perception of the market stays positive.

2) Foreign economies recover slowly *and* public perception of the market turns negative.

89.

3) Foreign economies prosper quickly, so fewer funds flow into U.S. markets *and* U.S. public perception of the market stays positive.

4) Foreign economies prosper quickly *and* public perception of the market turns negative.

These four simple scenarios vary in likelihood and each has different implications for the flow of funds into the market. They imply different courses of action investors should be prepared to undertake. They make it possible to monitor trends, watching key indicators to know which scenario is unfolding, and adjust investments accordingly.

A PROCEDURE FOR SCENARIO MAPPING

✔ Identify the variables or *dynamic factors* (positive and negative) you expect to exert the most influence on your organization, your markets and the attainment of your objectives.

✔ Consider *what might happen* within each dynamic factor during the time period of interest. Try five and ten-year horizons.

✔ Combine the dynamic factors into short stories about the future, creating a most-likely scenario, at least two extreme scenarios, and one or more middle-of-the-road scenarios.

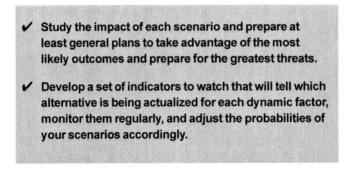

✔ Study the impact of each scenario and prepare at least general plans to take advantage of the most likely outcomes and prepare for the greatest threats.

✔ Develop a set of indicators to watch that will tell which alternative is being actualized for each dynamic factor, monitor them regularly, and adjust the probabilities of your scenarios accordingly.

There are two cautions to note about Scenario Mapping. One is the risk associated with sampling. You could create a nearly infinite variety of scenarios about the future, yet practicality limits you to examining only a few. How do you know you've chosen the right ones? The second caution is to recognize that this line of work mixes analysis and art—calling for considerable imagination and, at the same time, considerable judgment and common sense in choosing variables and crafting useful scenarios. The work calls for the most capable and talented team you can assemble.

End User Scenarios

"End User Scenarios are pictures that detail new benefits to users, the capabilities required to provide those benefits, and how the user interface will change."   –C.R. Snyder

Another analytic tool to consider in preparing for your strategy work is one we call End User Scenarios. It's a special type of scenario mapping that ties into Value Based Management and Inventing the Future.

End User Scenarios begin from extensive knowledge of those who buy and use your offerings, applying this knowledge as a foundation from which to picture the future. Many have found this technique useful, particularly those in rapidly developing, highly competitive, technology-driven markets.

Formal, large scale, end user research efforts are employed by many leading organizations. Toshiba and Sony, for example, both maintain substantial facilities dedicated to researching customer lifestyles. Their studies explore connections between the lifestyles of customers, the benefits that would enhance those lifestyles, and the technological innovations possible in future products/services.

You can explore these same connections through End User Scenarios. Naturally, this approach cannot supplant a large research program, yet it can, artfully executed, lead to rich, cost effective views of the future.

DEVELOPING END-USER SCENARIOS

✔ *Step 1: Collect Data.* End User Scenarios are founded on a deep knowledge of customers—who they are, how and why they choose your offerings, the functionalities and benefits they derive (in their own terms), the product/service characteristics they value and why, plus a full range of demographic variables.

✔ *Step 2: Create Prototype Users.* Segment your end users into groups. For those groups most important in the future, create prototype users by selecting appropriate lifestyle and demographic data points and fleshing out the pattern in short narratives that give names, lifestyle details, activities, etc.

✔ *Step 3: Create Benefit Scenarios.* For each prototype user, imagine details about the acquisition and use of your product/service. Consider its functionalities and benefits in the context of how the person lives. Consider future events, opportunities, and circumstances which may arise for the user. Write scenarios describing the functionalities, features and benefits and how they may contribute in the prototype user's life.

✔ *Step 4: Develop Implications.* Based on deep knowledge of the industry and emerging technologies, imagine future product/service offerings, connecting potential features and benefits with the life of the prototype end user. After you repeat the process by inventing several different end users (6 or more), look for the lessons that can be derived across your scenarios.

93.

Naturally, this technique must be used creatively and does not fit all circumstances. The basic idea is to establish a series of very specific customer models, each sufficiently tangible, rich, and detailed that you can readily imagine the impact of a certain feature or benefit on the person's life.

> *"What they [JVC, Apple, and others] saw was the potential to deliver new and profound customer benefits."*
> –G. Hamel & C.K. Prahalad

The value of End User Scenarios comes when they lead you to understanding new customer benefits for 2–10 years in the future. These benefits, in turn, imply certain capabilities and competencies you must have on board to actualize them. And finally, this kind of analysis leads you to reconsider, and perhaps modify, the user interface—meaning everything from the marketing and delivery of your offering to better "human engineering" the controls manipulated in using your product/service.

Part 5

Your Strategy Work

- Orchestrating the Process

- Preparation and Analysis

- Decision Making

- Activating Your Strategy

Orchestrating the Process

We've examined the leading concepts in strategy and several tools for strategy work. Now we turn to getting the work of strategy done in your organization.

Whether you're the only person in your enterprise officially responsible for strategy or a general manager wanting to upgrade your organization's work on strategy, you know that strategy is not a one-person job. When you are ready to initiate a strategy setting process, we believe you'll want to consider four things in getting started: *leader, workgroup, advisor,* and *process.*

1) **Leader.** While the work and accountability must be shared, someone must serve as the architect and focal point for getting strategy done.

2) **Workgroup.** The best strategy work often requires a group effort. While the workgroup may expand or contract throughout the process, it's best if certain core members participate throughout.

3) **Advisor.** Early on, you'll want to determine whether additional expertise will be helpful, an internal or external person to provide advisory, design, coaching, or technical support. If so, it's a good idea to get such a person involved at the very beginning.

4) **Process.** A process roadmap can keep your group on track and show the way to a successful conclusion.

More should be said about this last point, process. Strategy is commonly studied and revised during special workshops or retreats. These sessions allow time for concentrated effort and decision making and are, therefore, very helpful. However, your decision making constitutes only one portion of the total effort. Effective strategy implementation requires that decisions rely on solid analysis prepared beforehand and lead afterward directly into implementation activities. In short, your decisions must be part of a well-orchestrated process that begins some time before and extends some time after a planning retreat.

STRATEGY WORK PROCESS

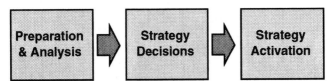

As noted earlier, we will not offer a detailed plan here, because your plan must be defined by someone with a closer knowledge of your business and circumstances. However, this simple three-stage process is a good starting point that fits many enterprises, SBU's and product groups.

Preparation and Analysis

"You can't hope to be lucky. You have to prepare to be lucky."
—Timothy Dowd

The purpose of this phase is to prepare for strategy deliberations and decision making, ensuring that the analytic work is complete and ready to use. This involves:

✔ Selecting the analyses that will be performed.

✔ Establishing a workgroup.

✔ Collecting and analyzing data.

✔ Preparing presentations.

Selecting Analyses. Earlier, we overviewed the conceptual building blocks of strategy and a select set of analytical tools. There's no formula for using these tools. You must select the concepts and tools that best fit your circumstances and become more familiar with them as needed. From these starting points, your analyses can be custom designed.

Establishing the Analysis Workgroup. The purpose of your workgroup is to gather facts, conduct necessary research and prepare appropriate presentations. These efforts will set the stage and frame the work of the strategy decision-making group. The group (often 3 or 4 individuals) should be guided by persons with appropriate experience as well as at least one very senior executive. The ideal workgroup is a diverse, cross functional group with good analytic and presentation skills.

Collecting and Analyzing Data. The assignments you give to the analysis workgroup will vary with your circumstances, but may include SWOT Analysis, Competitive Position Analysis, Scenarios, and other designs appropriate to your circumstances. The analyses will involve gathering facts and perhaps conducting original research on matters that range from operational effectiveness to the implications of emerging technologies. The work may include collecting data directly from customers as noted earlier.

Preparing Presentations. To ensure that the efforts of the analysis workgroup are fully useful, you'll want an integrated set of presentations prepared for the decision making sessions. It's vital that these presentations be visually effective, appropriate in detail, and integrated with one another in form and content. We find presentations are particularly powerful and compelling when they pair quantitative data, say on customer buying patterns, with qualitative data (quotes, stories, etc.) that make the same points.

Strategy Decisions

"You need people who can walk their companies into the future rather than back them into the future."
                                    –Warren Bennis

Whether you hold a single workshop or a series of planning sessions, in them you'll want to:

✔ Set the stage.

✔ Absorb the prepared analyses.

✔ Explore and decide key issues.

✔ Begin the strategy activation process.

Set the Stage. Early on, you'll want to introduce your purpose and agenda, lift the sights of the group away from daily details and get their strategic minds in gear by discussing fundamental principles of competitive strategy.

Absorb the Prepared Analyses. Present, discuss and digest the analyses prepared by the workgroup.

Explore and Decide Key Issues. Single out the issues that must be addressed, explore them efficiently, and arrive at decisions. Some of the matters you'll want to explore were outlined in the Work of Strategy chapter. A well-prepared facilitator, from inside or outside your organization, can usually help your decision-making group accomplish this work efficiently.

Apart from all the specific analyses and topics to be deliberated, at least three aspects of strategy should normally be addressed:

1) Your approach to competing for sales at the customer level.

2) The condition and position of your business vs. rivals.

3) The strategic initiatives and actions you will undertake to improve your position.

The first addresses how you'll compete for customers in the future, your future basis of competition. The second addresses the strengths and positioning of your organization among its peers and rivals on matters such as market share, competitive advantages, innovation, reputation, architecture, financial strength, operating efficiency, etc. The third addresses the measures you will undertake to achieve the basis of competition and the positioning versus rivals that you seek.

Begin Strategy Activation. Equally important to your strategy is the plan you set for implementing it. There is great symbolic and practical value in taking the initial steps to activate your strategy *during* your decision making session(s). This provides continuity and ensures the new direction is taken seriously.

Activating Your Strategy

"To manage strategy is to bridge thought into action."
—Richard Sessions

There's a long, unfortunate tradition of strategy as a planning exercise that never quite becomes day-to-day management. Realizing business results from your new or revised strategy means taking firm steps to activate it.

Ideally, your activation efforts should begin during your decision making session(s) and follow seamlessly into everyday work. How can that be done?

Activating strategy is like the proverbial three-legged stool. Each of its three elements must be in place for success. The three elements are accountability, metrics, and alignment.

THE THREE ELEMENTS OF ACTIVATION

Accountability. Accountability must be assigned and accepted for whatever strategic initiatives will implement your plan. Some initiatives, such as gaining market share

102.

through customer service, call for concerted action by many people. Others, such as consummating a key merger, call for action only by certain individuals and departments. Your particular strategy will call for accountabilities parceled out and designed to

"Action springs not from thought, but from a readiness for responsibility." –D. Bonheoffer

fit the players involved and the types of initiatives you set. Without properly set and managed accountabilities, strategic objectives typically dissolve into wishful thinking and spotty action.

Metrics. Measures and milestones are essential to effective strategy activation and often your most powerful mechanisms for converting a strategic concept into concrete reality. Metrics go a long way toward providing the gauges, levers, and handles to move your organization in the right direction.

Which metrics are best? First of all, balanced, strategy-based metrics. The Balanced Scorecard and similar designs are proven, effective tools for establishing tight linkage between your strategies and measures of performance.

The best scorecard from a management perspective will include at least two kinds of metrics. One kind gauges *business results* achieved. These measures are commonly called primary metrics, results measures, or lagging indicators. Traditional financial measures, such as *Earnings, ROI, Total Shareholder Return*, etc. are in this group. Such measures help you align efforts, manage accountabilities, track progress, and report results.

> *"A strategy without metrics is just a wish."* —E. Powell

The second kind of metric helps you manage performance day to day to achieve results—these are commonly called advanced metrics, drivers, leading indicators, or process measures. They track intermediate results, manage work processes, and improve capabilities to help you stop spinning wheels, avoid waste, get more output for your input, and prepare for the future. A companion volume in this series, *Measuring Performance* (Frost, 1998), addresses performance metrics.

Aligning Effort. Where your strategy calls for organization-wide action, initiatives must be cascaded to all appropriate levels. People must know about them; people must care about them; and people must be able to act on them.

Establishing these conditions calls for us to:

- ✔ **Translate.** Strategy must be translated into specific initiatives, accountabilities, and metrics.

- ✔ **Communicate.** Widespread understanding and commitment must be established. The importance of the

104.

new direction and the likely consequences of success or failure must be put forth convincingly and frequently.

✔ **Align.** "Vertical alignment" must be widely achieved in the organization.

More should be said about vertical alignment. It simply means that the objectives, goals, and efforts of every function and department are derived from, and aligned with, the direction and strategy of the enterprise. That's easy enough to say, but not so easy to achieve.

"Catchball" is one of several methodologies specifically designed for achieving vertical alignment. As initiatives are cascaded downward from one level to the next, they are redefined in terms of the accomplishments and measures of success expected. The receiving parties either accept the goals or negotiate modifications, based on resources required or barriers to be removed, before acceptance.

Without a process to intentionally produce vertical alignment, it's common to find departments and support groups setting goals and determining their initiatives with scarcely a glance toward the larger goals and strategies of the enterprise. We must help all departments see how their work fulfills a portion of the overall strategy and that, in fact, their goals are not valid without reference to the direction of the enterprise.

105.

Conclusion

"Business is like riding a bicycle. Either you keep moving or you fall down." —Frank Lloyd Wright

Well, in these few pages we've reviewed together the leading *concepts* in strategy, some useful *tools and methods*, and a *process* for getting the work done.

As you would expect in an overview book, most of what we've covered is well known to strategy practitioners and students of the literature. We've tried to summarize this body of work for you and, at the same time, fill certain gaps with ideas developed in our practice.

You may want to examine in more detail certain of the concepts and tools we have overviewed here. If so, you'll find the next chapter, References, a good starting point.

Throughout this book, we've repeated the message that your strategy, as well as your process for developing and refining it, must be specific to your organization and its unique characteristics and circumstances. We extend to you our best wishes in your work on this important matter.

References

Here are the works we've referenced in this book along with a few others you will find beneficial:

Day, G.S. *Market Driven Strategy.* New York, NY: Free Press, 1990. ISBN 0-02-907211-5.

Finnie, W.C. *Hands-On Strategy.* New York, NY: John Wiley & Sons, 1994. ISBN 0-471-04586-1.

Frost, B. *Measuring Performance: Using the New Metrics to Deploy Strategy and Improve Performance.* Dallas, TX: Measurement International. ISBN 0-7880-1407-2.

Grayson, C. J., Jr. and O'Dell, C. *American Business: A Two-Minute Warning.* New York, NY: The Free Press, 1988. ISBN 0-02-912680-0.

Hamel, G. and Prahalad, C.K. *Competing for the Future.* Boston, MA: Harvard Business School Press, 1994. ISBN 0-87584-416-2.

Kay, J.A. *Why Firms Succeed.* New York, NY: Oxford University Press, 1995.

Kay, J.A. *The Business of Economics.* New York, NY: Oxford University Press, 1996. ISBN 0-19-829-922-8.

Mintzberg, H. "Generic Strategies: Toward a Comprehensive Framework," in *Advances in Strategic Management*, R. B. Lamb & P. Shrivistava, eds., Greenwich, CT: JAI Press, 1988, pp. 1-67.

Ohmae, K. The Mind of the Strategist: The Art of Japanese Business. New York, NY: McGraw-Hill, 1982. ISBN 0-07-047904-6.

Porter, M.E. *The Competitive Advantage of Nations.* New York, NY: The Free Press, 1998. ISBN 0-6848-4147-9.

Porter, M.E. "How Competitive Forces Shape Strategy," *Harvard Business Review*, March-April, 1979.

Porter, M.E. "What Is Strategy?" *Harvard Business Review*, November-December, 1996.

Schwartz, P. *The Art of the Long View.* New York, NY: Doubleday, 1991. ISBN 0-385-26732-0.

Tregoe, B.B. and Zimmerman, J.W. *Top Management Strategy: What It Is and How to Make It Work.* New York, NY: Simon and Schuster, 1980. ISBN 0-671-25401-4.

A final note. . .

We hope you find this book useful in your strategy work. Please be aware that Measurement International makes several types of supporting services available to those implementing the concepts in this book. You can reach Measurement International at 214-350-1082.

Additional copies. . .

For fast service on additional copies of this book, or others in this series, you can copy this page and fax to 214-350-1083, or phone the publisher at 214-350-1082.

Number of copies required: _____

Name: _____

Title: _____

Company: _____

Address: _____

City, State, ZIP: _____

Phone:_____ E-mail:_____

Orders direct from the publisher are priced at $12.00 per copy, plus shipping / handling of $2.50 per copy for delivery in the United States. Additional charges apply for international delivery and for sales tax on orders in the state of Texas. Credit card payments are welcome.